Contents

Introduction

This ten step action plan is written for everyone wanting to improve their current job situation. The harsh reality is that over 80%* of the work force strongly dislike or at the worst hate their job. The purpose and intention of this book is to assist you who are in this group wanting to improve to get to a place where you are fulfilled and happy with your job situation, not having to fear if you are going to survive, if your situation will not improve or have to experience discomfort when someone asks you what you do for a living. The focus of this guide is on the so-called "Hidden Job Market", which constitutes for over 80% of all jobs. These are the jobs that are never advertized and where you stand the strongest to be successful. All information and guidance conveyed is based on my own personal experience as an international corporate headhunter for the last two decades working on more than 3500 recruitments, which has involved interviewing and assessing more than 10,000 job candidates. Since 1997, I´ve been the CEO of a successful international headhunter company I founded and still preside, with offices in Europe and US. I have also written several books, this including a bestseller targeting executive search firms on how to find the candidates they are seeking. My firm's clients are solely corporations, never job candidates. My company never makes money from job candidates, as we are always paid by our clients with the need of filling the job positions. This guide is based on how the job market really works, and how people like me; a corporate recruiter, or a hiring company would conduct their hiring and how you can succeed by learning these secrets. Being a strong believer in people, I believe that everyone has the potential to turn their job and life situation around,

despite an economy with fewer jobs openings than in the past. I also want to emphasize that unless someone is willing to adapt to the necessary mindset and do whatever it takes to succeed, no change or improvement can be expected. With great uncertainties of if and when things will get better in the economy, or if the same jobs will be around in the future, nobody can afford to passively wait for things to get better. A new way of thinking is therefore necessary if what you are doing now isn´t working out. Always keep in mind: everything can be fixed, ranging from you being a part of an excess labor force with skills no longer in demand, not possessing the skills for the jobs that are now in demand, or simply stuck in a job you strongly dislike. Your success depends both on you knowing how to best maneuver to both get a job, and progress in one, but equally, if not even more importantly, the need of you being "pro-active" and how good you are at integrating into your life, nurturing the listed four essential core traits;

Imagination Creating new ways and solutions require imagination
Vision You need to know what you want and desire, which is a specific goal
Collaboration Success is always a result of a team effort, this being networking, or at work.
Fearlessness Overcoming fear is essential, as it's one of the key reasons to what you keep doing what is not working

With a change of mindset and integrating the necessary information presented in this 10 step guide, you will have a very strong chance at being successful in job market, regardless of your current situation. When following this guide is important to not just to believe you will succeed, but knowing it, as your life reflects your state of mind and thereby the degree of success you will achieve.

TEN STEP ACTION PLAN FOR MASTERING YOUR JOB/CAREER

As you follow each of these steps, do so with the understanding that getting a job, keeping the job you have, or improving your career situation must be approached with dedication, perseverance, and determination. This is not just about getting a paycheck; it's about developing this part of your life in alignment with the talents of your true self. It's about being proud to be the best you can be. Only then will you approach the work you do with passion and enthusiasm and be able to keep it in balance with the other four key areas of your new life.

Step One: Assess your current job/career situation
While assessing your job/career situation you must be completely honest with yourself; otherwise you're wasting your time and won't get positive results. Answer these questions:

• Do you have a job?
• Do you want to be more successful in the job you currently have?
• Did you lose your job?
• Do you fear losing your job?
• Why are things not working out both now and in the past? ("I don't know" is not an acceptable answer! If you can't figure it out, who will?)

Step Two: Assess yourself as an employee/potential employee *Would you hire or promote yourself? Why/why not?*
Look at yourself from the perspective of an employer who may consider

hiring you, or your current employer who may promote you, when so many other people are competing in a tough job market.

The first question you should ask yourself is if you would hire or promote yourself, and why/why not. This test will help you determine where you stand today, and also give you important information about what you need to change about yourself. Bottom line: if you would not hire or promote yourself, why should someone else do it? Answer these questions as objectively as possible:

1) Are you a person who radiates positive energy, and people want to be around you due to your 24/7 upbeat attitude/personality?
2) Are you a high energy, hard worker who always wants to exceed expectations by doing your very best no matter what your assignment?
3) Are you a person who always takes the initiative, rather than having to be asked to do things?
4) Are you independent and self-driven, meaning once you get going you don't need much input from your superior?
5) Are you always looking out for your boss or company's best interests rather than your own?
6) Outside of official work hours do you find ways to learn more in order to excel at your work, such as by reading, taking higher education classes, and seminars, etc.?
7) Are you always dressed and groomed professionally so that if clients dropped by you would be a good role model for the company?
8) Are you always loyal and dependable to your company?

If you answered "yes" to all of the questions above, you should not hesitate to hire yourself. On the other hand, if you answered "no" to any of the questions, you need to examine yourself further and change your thinking and behavior as soon as possible. The truth is, during over 3,500 recruitments I have conducted as a headhunter, not once has a client said, "Find me a lazy, rude, dishonest, repulsive, unstable job candidate with no drive and initiative." If someone wants to strongly stand out in the job market they better answer yes to all of the eight questions above. By being all you can be you will always be needed and wanted in the job market.

What are your unique skill sets and talents?
When you are looking for a job, first of all it's important for you to be "hire-able." Before you can honestly tell a potential employer that you're the best person for the job they're seeking to fill—or convey such confidence during a job interview—you must know the skills and talents you would bring to the job. If you want to be more successful in your current job, you must understand how your unique skill sets and talents could be put to better use.

Make a list of all of your skills and talents, including everything you have learned to do through your education, training, or work experience, as well as things you naturally do well. How could those talents be used in a job or career?

What can you do to improve your chances or opportunities? To spark the interest of any company/business, you need a written onepage presentation of yourself (your bio/résumé) showing why you are a good bet. The past usually sets the standard for the future. Still, it's never too late to change if you're not happy with your life and what you've accomplished up to this point. I believe we all have it in us to greatly improve and radically change our lives at any point we choose. This being said, the way the corporate world works is that when you apply for a job, your bio, which is your life story, sets a prediction for the future and how well, or not well, you will do in a new job. Being a great talker isn't enough if your talk does not match your bio. In fact, it's easy for a professional who might be interviewing you to quickly perceive "fluff," meaning lots of smoke and no action.

Your bio/résumé: A bio/résumé usually doesn't lie and it seldom undersells —it's intended to do the opposite. It needs to be short and precise, with everything summarized on one page. It should nail in chronological order in bullet-point format each job you have had, including this information:

- the name of the company
- your job position or title
- the time period you worked there
- a short description of the company (size, products/services, etc.)
- your key work tasks
- the name of your supervisor

A separate section should include your education, where you went to school, dates you attended, GPAs, and degrees earned.

If your bio/résumé does not at least get you an interview, then you're on thin ice and either need to take out what could be viewed as negatives or consider adding side projects that are relevant to the type of job you are seeking. Red flags on a bio/résumé are gaps between jobs or attending school—which show lack of incentive or laziness— and too many jobs in a short time period —which show instability—and no progression of accomplishments in your work history. Positive additions to a bio/ résumé include side interests that make you seem vibrant and can easily trigger conversations between standard questions during a job interview, creating a more personal interaction. But don't overdo. Too many outside interests can imply that they are more important than your job, which is a strong negative.

A strong bio/résumé sums up your life and how it has been used so far. I always like to ask people if they are happy with their accomplishments. If they are it means he/she is living according to a set plan versus someone who lives on chance with no direction. Your bio/résumé should also reflect anything unique about you that required sacrifice, such as night or weekend classes or schooling or independent projects to advance your skill set in your chosen career field. Better still is when a person's outside activities and background show ways they devote time to helping others without getting paid. But again, do not overdo. These extra activities strongly help you stand out, but only if they do not give the impression they will take away from or interfere with your job by putting a burden on your time or energy. The main objective when hiring someone to do a job is that he/she can and will do the best possible job and make the greatest possible impact on the company. Very few companies tolerate employees who neglect their duties for whatever reasons, even by doing goodwill extracurricular activities.

Your bio/résumé may need to be tweaked to specifically reflect the skills, experiences, and knowledge you have that make you ideally suited for a particular job you are seeking. But don't allow yourself to be caught up in endlessly rewriting your bio/résumé. That type of procrastination is often the result of fear of rejection. Don't allow it into your consciousness. Just forge ahead with your best efforts. A little extra time tailoring your bio/résumé could make the difference by getting you an interview.

Also, never forget that your bio/résumé is just part of your presentation. Your interview is another part (which will be discussed shortly). When someone expresses an interest in hiring you, they will check your references from previous employers. Never list your references on your bio/résumé, but instead use a notation saying references will be provided upon request. You don't want your references to receive too many phone calls from people inquiring about you, or else they may become weary of responding and their glowing recommendations could become less enthusiastic.

Perhaps you now understand that everything you have done in your life, every choice you have made, will contribute to the opportunities and choices made available to you in the future. If you feel you have already fallen short, don't be discouraged—no one is perfect. Although you can't change the past, you can begin today to live with integrity in alignment with your true self, building a future with unlimited potential for happiness and fulfillment.

Step Three: Decide your job/career future in specific terms Create a future bio/résumé for the following time frames: twelve months from now, three years from now, and five years from now.

When you want something in life, it's important to set a clear goal in order to achieve it. First, set a realistic target, but allow yourself to dream. Set a high goal that requires you to really stretch in order to reach it—this could mean you need to acquire a certain skill set or knowledge. Then ask yourself why you want to reach this goal? Is it because you want to test yourself to see how far you can go? Or is it because you feel the new knowledge or position will give you a certain feeling of accomplishment? Maybe it's because you feel you can better serve a higher purpose by being able to help more people with your gifts or help them in a better way. The reasons can be many, but it's important to know why, because your reasons are the key to your passions (motivation).

Second, in order to stay motivated you need to set milestones: small

goals with steps to take in order to reach each one of them. My own personal experience is that I would not have reached any of my goals in life if I had not set a clear path to follow. Everything I have achieved in my life—and has been achieved in the lives of the candidates I have recruited—resulted from planning and hard work. Little in life falls into someone's lap unexpectedly. Life planning and time management are needed for each of the five key areas of life, including job/career. Planning does not mean you stop living for today and start believing everything in the future will be so much greater. The only reason to make plans is to ensure you get the most of this life. Remember to shoot for the stars, but never forego the principles of life balance, which are required in order to live a Second Life.

Step Four: Decide on a job/career action plan and timelines according to your future bio/résumé
Once you have set clear goals for your job/career you need to decide on an effective plan of action to achieve what you want.

• Will you stay in your current job?
• If you have no job:
a) Are you willing to accept a temporary job while you pursue your

dream job or work toward getting it?
b) Do you plan to wait it out until you get the "right job"? If so:
• Decide on a timeline. How long will it take to achieve your goal?
• Define your approach. How will you get the job you want? How

much time are you willing to allocate for your job search?

Many people believe it's better to spend an extensive period of time looking for a job where they can utilize their talents and get on a career track, rather than accepting a temporary mediocre job that may not advance their career, or a job considered a "second grade job" according to society's standards. This is a belief system based on ego and indoctrination that limits job opportunities and growth. When you really need a job, this type of thinking will defeat you. If jobs in your chosen field are scarce, it's far better for your state of mind, as well as your financial situation, to find the best job you can for the time being and do the best work you can at that job—until you can get back on your career track.

Step Five: Decide how important a job/career is to you
Evaluate what is important in regard to job/career versus other activities in your life by listing them in order of importance. Then ask yourself how much you are willing to sacrifice in order to get where you want to go in your job/career. And ask yourself why.

Years ago when there was no welfare, as there is today, or money from parents coming your way—with which you could "buy time"— getting a job as opposed to having a career was more geared toward the following order: 1) Survival—any job that could pay your bills would do. 2) A career—a job where you could utilize your talents and fully grow was a luxury.

Survival mode is no longer predominant in the current belief system. Today people are programmed to a great extent to believe everything will work itself out, that finding "the right job" is better than accepting a job defined by society as "degrading." This, again, makes people feel like they are judged by what they do for a living instead of who they are. Maslow's Hierarchy of Needs was a key driving force in the past. And today, despite society's standards, Maslow's principle—which clearly indicates our first need in life is survival—still holds true. Then comes personal growth and fulfillment.

Work builds character

If someone is healthy with a working mind there is no reason whatsoever that they can- not be an active contributor to our society. If someone is able to make a contribution, they should do so in some capacity. If their situation does not allow for a career track job, then a temporary job will have to do. If it's difficult to obtain a temporary job, then some sort of project can be embarked upon. This could be anything ranging from helping people in the community to an internship to obtain more knowledge and experience, enabling them to have a better chance in the job market. The key is to be active in one way or another.

There was a time when teens and young adults had to work while growing up. They had duties and responsibilities at home and got jobs during their time off from school in the summer. As a result, they learned discipline, developed character, and understood survival mode. Now, unfortunately, there is a completely different mindset.

Recruiters and employers always look at what people have done in the past as an indication of their futures because they know character development does not happen over night, but comes with experience and molding. They look for a person who knows what work means because such people are usually more disciplined—a trait they developed by working rather than getting handouts. Discipline is an extremely important attribute to have in order to succeed in the workforce. Nobody wants to hire a person who does not have the discipline to arrive at work on time in the morning and stay until the job is done.

The hiring process is always about reducing risks—meaning a company would rather hire someone who has a steady job history with good references, rather than someone who has been "hanging out," or frequently changing jobs. Future employers do not like to hear too many explanations of "why this and that" did not work out in the past.

Step Six: Determine how you can contribute to making the world a better place by using the gifts/talents of your true self in the workplace In his inaugural address in 1961, President John F. Kennedy implored citizens of the United States: "Ask not what your country can do for you, but what you can do for your country." This motivation can easily be transferred to the corporate world—and all of life, in fact. We have been indoctrinated to wait for a clear sign about what benefits we will receive from our employer before doing something outside of our job description. The mentality is often: How will you reward me if I do such and such? The opposite way of thinking is to first think about what you can do for your company. Every employer likes this attitude because it clearly shows a team spirit; that you are not a person driven purely by the ego, but by something greater than yourself.

This approach and attitude, of course, needs to leave room and time for you to still have a balance between work and off time (time to recharge). But in order to grow and advance in your career, you need to put something in before you'll get something back. It's not possible to have it both ways. Your goal is not to feed your ego by always questioning what the company, your colleagues or others can do for you. True fulfillment comes by finding ways you can be of service to others.

Honor your true self—Be all you can be
Each of us has been provided with unique gifts and talents that are endlessly beyond anything we can grasp—resources we need to tap into and develop as much as possible. By doing so you will be able to find ways to give back to others and serve a higher purpose with your talents, which is the true meaning of life.

The reality is, many people feel just "keeping it together" sometimes seems like a huge challenge. They barely have enough time or energy to get through the daily duties required just to maintain their existence. Clearly, how we use our time makes all the difference. When it comes to our jobs or careers there will always be choices to make about how we use our passions or invest our time. These choices are based on how we view our jobs/careers in perspective to our entire lives. Is your job/career a part of all that your life should be? Or does it define everything you are?

No matter what job/career situation you are in, always honor your true self. Do your very best and be grateful you are healthy, able to work, and have a job at all. By being grateful you show respect to the greatest gift of all, *life*, knowing deep inside that you are doing your best to be all you can be in life. As a recruiter I never pay much attention to what people do for a living, but rather how much effort and commitment they put into their work and themselves, which is demonstrated by how they carry themselves. Respect comes through these things, not by what you do. People who possess these positive traits are the ones who make me feel good when I meet them; they enlighten my day. As a recruiter these are also the people I am always looking to recruit, because I know they have what it takes to truly succeed in life. These are the people who, no matter where you find them currently, will succeed because nothing can stop them when they are living according to how their true self wants them to live.

If a man is called a street sweeper, he should sweep streets as Michelangelo painted, or Beethoven composed music, or Shakespeare wrote poetry. He should sweep streets so well that all the hosts of heaven and earth will pause to say: Here lived a great street sweeper who did his job well.

Martin Luther King, Jr.

Step Seven: Learn the realities of the corporate world
How does the corporate world work and operate in regard to the mentality, procedures, and what it takes to succeed and excel? What's the difference between a "rising star" and a "warm body filling a chair"?

Knowledge is power. In many occupations, what you know, as well as what you are continually learning, will to a great extent determine your worth. A person who has acquired the right knowledge and skill set stands out and competes on a different level than others in the job market. Securing or keeping your job/career isn't enough. You must always continue to learn in order to grow that aspect of your life, which contributes to your being a fully realized whole person.

Many people say they don't have the time after work hours of their primary job to study on their own, attend school, or commit to a parttime job to expand their base of knowledge or skills. The truth is, most people do have the time, but they've decided to spend it on nonproductive activities, such as watching television. Life is about priorities and how you use your minutes on earth. You can invest them by learning, growing, and evolving or you can choose to waste them. A recent survey showed that an average American has watched 15 years of television by the time they reach the age of 60—which is 15 years wasted! Looking back on your life from the vantage point of your twilight years, what activities enriched your life more?

Educate yourself. Instead of watching television or wasting your valuable minutes in other non-constructive ways, take advantage of them by reading about your chosen career, attending classes, networking with others in your field, or brainstorming with other smart people or with yourself while taking a walk or getting some healthy outdoor exercise. Your opportunities to learn and grow are as limitless as your potential.

Learning and growing = utilizing the gifts of your true self to the fullest— which is why we are blessed with mind and body. By wasting time we are disgracing your true self. Our duty is to live a balanced, whole life by being all we can be, which we do by constantly learning throughout life in order to never stop growing and discovering our full potential.

Reality check: The company needs you only as long as you are making money for them. They are not your friends
Although you most certainly will develop friendships, and perhaps strong personal ties with your coworkers, always remember that we live in a capitalistic world where profit needs to be generated in order for a company to survive and evolve. When this is not accomplished there will be no security for you in your job.

The reason someone has hired you for a job is because you are the machinery for creating profit and sustaining it. You are needed only as long as this is taking place. Unless you can create an added value, you are a liability— which means you are at risk of losing your job because you are not needed. So always remember that the only reason you were hired and remain on the job is because directly or indirectly you can create profit. The more you are able to the create and contribute to the profits of the company by being a high performer and role model, the more likely you are to have job security.

Despite the fact that the company—your employer—is not your family or your friend, it doesn't mean you should be lax in making a contribution to creating a pleasant environment; but it means to never be blind to the truth, no matter how cozy it seems around you. If you don't perform or your company is doing poorly, you will be eliminated. Even if your superiors like you, remember that they have bosses they are accountable to, who has a boss, etc., etc., etc. Every employee is just a replaceable element in a greater system, which has dominance over everything else in order to survive and thrive. It's not personal. This is the market mechanism that determines who and what has the right to exist through natural growth and sustainability, and who and what does not.

Keeping this in mind, never forget that you don't owe anything to anyone. If you leave for a better job somewhere else, you someone will replace you who can do the job at least as well as you can, perhaps even better; otherwise the company will not survive and/or thrive. But if you are given an opportunity to grow and evolve to the next level in the company/corporation where you're currently employed, take advantage of the opportunity.

Your job insurance policy: Don't be naive
Wherever you're working, always know that your purpose is to serve a function for a company/corporation that needs to make a profit. It's Economics 101. Their benefits (profits) for having you there must exceed what it costs them to keep you—although in some job situations it's more difficult to calculate your personal cost/benefits ratio because you function as part of a team and your contribution can't be separated from the team as a whole.

When things are pointing upward in the economy and your employer's business is doing well, you'll have a job as long as your supervisor and coworkers are happy with you and your performance. But when things turn downward in the economy or people around you are not satisfied with you or your work, you are on thin ice. In a good economy, people who don't perform as well are more likely to get away with it than they are during an economic downturn. Not being a worker of excellence in a bad economy means you'll be the first to go. Your insurance policy is not to be naïve. Despite how cozy and friendly your job environment may seem, the company you are working for is there to create a profit and you are there to make it happen. Therefore, they will rapidly eliminate your position if your services are no longer needed. The sooner you realize this, the better.

In addition to always working hard and smart, to safeguard your position, keep any dissatisfaction you feel with your current job—such as coworker incompatibilities or your need for higher pay or advancement—to yourself unless you believe the problems you're having can be solved. If they can, make an appointment with your supervisor/boss specifically for the purpose of discussing your current position and your potential for future growth and advancement. During such a meeting, any problems you face and have been unable to resolve on your own can be an item on the agenda, but they should never be the expressed purpose for the meeting—otherwise your supervisor/boss will be put in a defensive position instead of in a problem-solving position and you may be viewed as a troublemaker.

Many people who are dissatisfied with their jobs or have problems that can't be solved begin looking for a new job. Good move. But then they feel a strong need to confide to their boss when they are job searching. They don't realize is that by doing so, they have broken the main rule, which is trust. The boss is not family and the fact is, an employee already has a foot out the door says loud and clear that something is not working properly. Or the boss may suspect the reason they've been told is a ploy to elicit a salary increase or a promotion. Put frankly, this is a bad way to operate and is equal to blackmail because any salary raise or promotion offered under such circumstances has not been achieved in a fair manner. Either of the two situations described is grounds for dismissal at the first crossroad.

Looking at the long term, you never want to burn bridges. If you're looking for a new job, do so discreetly; never let anyone else at your current company know. Secondly, if your present employer/boss knows you're out there looking—and doesn't fire you—it means he or she will be contacted for a reference check by anyone considering hiring you— something that's close to impossible if you run the process off the radar. Think about it. Would you want the company you're hoping to leave be a main source of information for a potential new employer?

During my long career as a high-level headhunter and life coach, I am almost always working with those who believe they owe it to their bosses to tell him/her when they are in the process of looking for a different job. Or they say they can't leave their present company because they "owe them so much." Loyalty is a worthy attribute, but it's a mistake to believe the company/corporation where you work would have the same consideration for you if it were in their best interest to replace you or eliminate your job. My answer to anyone who expresses such a sentiment is: Your highest authorities in life is your god and your country; next is you and your family, then comes the company/ corporation employing you.

When your challenges at your current job are not insurmountable and your own problem solving, combined with the efforts of coworkers and your supervisor/boss seem to be improving the situation, it may be best to stay where you are. But even then—or when you actually feel happy and fulfilled with your work—still know that your company is not your family. Be prepared at all times, just in case something happens and one day you find out you won't be working there anymore. This means, always have your résumé ready, and never be naïve—you can't afford to be.

Step Eight: Execute your job/career action plan to get where you want to go by getting a new job or making your job all it can be

Getting a new job
Where do you find a job? There are various places to look for a job. The easiest place to look is where the chances of succeeding are the lowest. So don't take the easy way out. Getting a job must always be viewed as a job itself. It requires a game plan, a methodical process with a sequence of events you follow.

First, understanding the job market helps you understand your odds. What types of job searches lead to most people successfully finding a job? The statistics shows that a majority of all jobs—over 80 percent— are never advertised and only a small portion of the job market is covered through the classifieds in newspapers and on the Internet, which is called the hidden job market. An even smaller amount of jobs are obtained through recruiters.

As with everything else in life, the harder and smarter you work, the better your results will be. So it's best to spend most of your time on approaches that will give you the most positive results. When looking for a job, allocate almost your entire time to taking a direct approach. This doesn't mean you should ignore other approaches that are statistically less fruitful. Prioritize according to importance. While conducting your targeted direct job search, still check the classified ads and check in with your network for opportunities, but keep the time spent on these activities to a minimum every day as you need most of your energy and focus to go toward being proactive and approaching your target companies directly.

How to best approach a job opportunity: Be proactive
Although being approached by a headhunter is the best thing that could happen to you, unfortunately the chances of this happening are usually slim because only a fraction of the jobs are being channeled through this source.

Your next best maneuver is to be proactive. First, identify the potential companies where you would like to work. But, of course, be realistic. It's important to understand what you can bring to the table. If you have no knowledge or skills in the field of computer technology, the chances of your scoring a high-paying job with great benefits at Microsoft or Google as a programmer or technician are slim to none. So don't waste your time or theirs.

Ask yourself: What unique skill set or knowledge do I have that the company I am approaching needs? Getting a job is similar to sales: it's a numbers game. The product you are selling is yourself. Just like in sales, the more potential buyers you have who need the services you are selling, the better your chances of success. Few prospects and bad buyers—those who don't need your services, for example, Google, if you're a medical technician not a computer tech—means your chances of getting anywhere are slim. On the other hand, if you are realistic about how your skills and knowledge (reflected on your bio/résumé) could be of benefit to certain companies, you have just as good a chance as anyone else to get your foot in the door.

Another consideration is geography. Are you willing to move to another place or do you prefer to stay local? Although commuting might be an option, most employers and headhunters know that even if a candidate claims he/she will have no problem driving two hours each way, the reality has proven to be that after a few months, commuting takes it toll.

Now that you've identified the type of companies that can use your skills and knowledge and you've decided on a geographical area, what do you do next? You are going to contact the companies by telephone, a personal visit, or email—but always know you are not alone in doing so. There are lots of other people doing the exact same thing. This is where a good bio/résumé comes into play. The time you have put into polishing and tailoring your bio/résumé could make the difference. But again, don't let polishing/tailoring your bio/résumé become an excuse for not moving forward. Just like with anything else, the more you do it the easier it will be. Just keeping doing it!

In good times when there are fewer applicants for available jobs, companies and recruiters pay more attention to unsolicited bio/résumés. But when times are tough, with fewer jobs available, it's an entirely different story. Then the best chance you have when approaching companies directly is to make sure you stand out—without, of course, being "a stalker." Develop and keep a proactive mindset. Even though some people will think you're too aggressive, this isn't relevant if out of a hundred companies you approach, you get noticed by all of them— who now know you exist—and ten invite you in for an interview.

When I was starting out, I looked for jobs in both Europe and the United States and tried every approach I could think of. I sent applications in response to ads in the classifieds and tried to use my network. Neither did much for me. But when I used my direct approach, compiling my list and hitting the pavement, I always succeeded. All of my own job opportunities resulted from this proactive approach.

Here's a game plan: Use a system I call mapping, a systematic method to be as efficient as possible.

• Make a list in a table format (preferably on the computer) with four columns.
• In the first column put the name of each company (it's best to put them in alphabetical order—easy to do on a computer), their address, and main telephone number.
• In column two put the name of your contact person, their direct dial phone number, and email address.
• The third column is for you to note the dates when you take each action step.
• Column four is where you will write notes of status and next steps.

Again, don't put too much time into creating your list. If you get hung up on doing so, consider whether it's a form of procrastination. The point here is not to spend all of your time creating the list, but to use your time finding a job!

Before you start mailing/emailing your résumé, create the best possible prospect list you can. This should take no longer than a couple of days. You can use the Internet for identifying the companies (as well as their addresses and main phone numbers), but do not use it for determining the key people you are going to directly contact. The most accurate and quickest way to get the information is by calling. Yes, you guessed it. You will not be contacting the human resources department, but finding out the name of the person in each company who is in charge of the department that could benefit from hiring you based on your skills. Call the main phone number of each company and ask who has such responsibility. As examples, if you are in sales, ask for the name of the person who heads up the sales department. Or, if you are in accounting, ask for the name of the person in charge of the accounting department.

Keep in mind that the higher you go in the organization, the more authority that person has to make a hiring decision. The lower you go, the more reluctant those people will be to make a decision—a wrong hiring decision, particularly at lower levels of the hierarchy of a company, might mean that person is putting their own job at jeopardy (you don't need another person out there competing with you for a job).

Although many companies like to have job seekers filtered through their HR (human resources) departments, my personal experience is that if you have to deal with HR—as opposed to approaching the head of an appropriate (for you) department of the company—you're more likely to have your bio/résumé end up in a fi ling cabinet. And, by the way, when you get a personalized letter stating: "Thank you for your letter. We are impressed with your background, but have no current needs matching your qualifications. We will get back to you when an opening arises," this most likely means you will never hear from them again. This is, quite frankly, because the people sending these types of letters to you and other job applicants have more than enough on their plates and are just doing their best to stay on top of their current responsibilities. Usually they do not have time to keep track of all the people applying for jobs.

Also know that although the HR department may be "filtering" job applicants, many aren't authorized to do the hiring. The people who actually do the hiring are department heads or managers in areas of the business where you want to work. Hiring is part of their responsibilities. Someone who runs a business area or is an upper-level manager of a department wants to recruit the very best people for his or her team to ensure the department maintains a high level of performance.

Once you've completed your list, it's time to systematically get your résumé out there. Email it first, then call, then follow up again, and keep doing it until closure takes place. My own practice to make sure my bio/ résumé hit its target was to use all the means available to me: phone, fax and email just to make sure. This way the people you are contacting can never say, "I am sorry, I did not get your résumé/letter/message." Just as if you are working in sales, you have not closed the deal until you get a job—and even then you are not safe until you physically start working, because sometimes job offers are rescinded after they are offered.

Remember, getting a job is a numbers game. The bigger and better your approach, the greater your chances are of winning. A job search process is no different than a sales approach. The key rule is: the chances of someone knocking on your door with an opportunity of a lifetime is close to zero. This means you have to do the work and use the techniques that work the best—which from my experience is the proactive direct approach. As I said before, if some of the companies you contact think you're too aggressive, don't worry about it. Other companies will assume that if you are a go-getter when it comes to getting the job, then you will use that same enthusiasm, follow-through, and energy once you start working for them. Remember: The harder you hit it the better your chances of success.

It may be temping to take the easy way out, by sending off some emails based on classified ads, posting your résumé online, or sending blind résumés to a lot of different companies. But that's identical to thinking that going to the gym and putting in five minutes of work will get you the body of your dreams, or by buying a lottery ticket at 7-Eleven you'll become financially independent. It just does not work like that. It's better to understand right from the start that you always spend 95 percent of your time where you believe you have a 95 percent chance to succeed, and only 5 percent of your time where there is only a 5 percent chance of success. There are no shortcuts to nailing your dream job. By giving it your best and rolling up your sleeves, you can get what you want—the job you deserve—and also know you always put forth your best effort and it's all you can do. That way of living is honoring your true self!

The job interview process is like the dating game
Although a good bio/résumé is key to getting your foot in the door, in reality it doesn't show a potential employer who you really are as a person or what it would be like to have you around the office every day—your personality and attitude. That will come through during your job interview.

When you are invited to a job interview it means your chances of getting the job are great. After all, why would they waste their valuable time talking to you unless they believe there is a good chance you might be the right candidate for the job? My experience is, if you've succeeded in getting all the way to a face-to-face meeting with your potential new employer, then your skills meet their requirements and the rest is really up to you. Nine out of ten people can shift the outcome of an interview toward acceptance, rather than rejection, if they really understand what it means to be invited to a job interview. Someone who gets the opportunity to meet with a future employer usually either nails it or messes it up in the first few minutes. When prospective employees with great qualifications still mess it up it's usually because they don't have what I like to call the right "human touch." They do not know how to properly walk, talk, and behave around others—and someone else did.

This can easily be changed by turning it around, looking at it from the perspective of the person conducting the interview. Before a job interview, visualize yourself in the shoes of the interviewer. What impressions do you need to get from someone seeking a job? What questions are you most likely to ask and what answers do you want to hear? Beyond that, what posture do you want to see, what kind of speech pattern do you want to hear, and what kind of handshake do you want to feel?

Unfortunately 99 percent of people do not spend time imagining they are in the interviewer's position, which causes them to not nail it during their job interviews. As a recruiter I do feel bad when this happens. I see people who fail despite having the potential and the right background, because they are not able to nail that one meeting that could dramatically change their life for the better. (Lack of preparation can be reflected, not just in the job market, but also in all areas of life.)

When it comes to preparing for a job interview it's of great importance to practice, practice, and practice even more. First imagine yourself in the role of the interviewer. Then become who you are, the job seeker, and practice how you will show your potential new employer that you're the right person (i.e., personality and attitude) for the job.

Practice until it all sticks and becomes an integrated part of you. Another golden rule of a job interview is that it's a two-way street— meaning you are there to sell yourself to the company and the company is trying to sell itself to you. It's all about structure with a natural flow. One key is to find common ground—so you don't sound like a programmed robot. Do some research to learn about the person who will be interviewing you by Googling him or her —but tell the person where you learned about him or her, otherwise you might sound like a stalker. Glance around the interviewer's office to find items indicate areas of common interests: memorabilia, photographs, artwork, books, etc. Make nice comments. Stay positive, upbeat, high-energy, polite, and courteous. Bottom line, be prepared and know the questions and answers before you arrive, be likeable, and nail it by being the person you know they would love to hire—you!

Learn the answers and questions before the interview
When you practice before a meeting with a potential employer and you are going through potential questions and answers it's important to understand that these questions are usually very universal. Always know, the purpose of the meeting is to get to know you better than your onepage bio/résumé can present, have you elaborate on your skill set, and figure out if you are a high flyer, go-getter, or just a "warm body" who will make no additional contribution outside of minimal expectations.

Many job candidates get easily tricked or just don't know that if a conversation appears casual it does not mean they don't need to stay on point and cover the key information needed. Many times I have seen job seekers be thrown off-balance when a potential employer asks a question about a hobby or non-work-related activity in the middle of the conversation. They start talking about such things and are unable to get back to the real topic at hand:

the work done by the company and how they can make a valuable contribution. The sad reality is, when you're invited for an interview, that's your only chance to get the job. It's the same story as when a salesperson spends weeks setting up a meeting to present the company's product or services, and then messes up the one window of opportunity. It's totally unacceptable to screw up the conversation.

In the final analysis, preparation is what will determine if you are in or out, so every minute spent getting ready is worth it.

Many companies prefer a less casual, more structured interview process. They start by asking a job candidate to tell more about himself/ herself— occasionally breaking into the conversation with questions— then switch during the second half of the interview to talking about the job and their company. Other times it might be in the reverse order, but what never changes are the key pieces of information that need to be covered.

One of the flaws I often see is when job candidates are asked to tell more about themselves and they do so too quickly, often in only five minutes. This makes the interviewer question what kind of life this person has if they can describe it in such a short time. And when job candidates focus completely on their skill sets and say nothing about who they are as people they can lose their potential new employer before they're halfway through.

Every company considers it a great test to see how effectively a job candidate is able to communicate when presenting himself/herself. During the late 1990s, several seminars cropped up to help people get a job—at least that's what it seemed, as I meet a number of people who would talk about themselves in the third person. This approach and method killed anyone's chance in less than two minutes. These job candidates would insist on using a Powerpoint presentation while referring to themselves in this way: "What Tom wants and needs are . . ." When I heard this I always knew what Tom needed . . . and that was to leave.

Another interesting attitude and approach I have seen is when someone— meaning a job candidate—enters the room in a cocky manner, sits down with his/her arms crossed and starts the conversation by just saying, "Sell me." When this has happened I have told these people politely that there is a mismatch, because I know for certain they should not be involved in any job process.

These are examples of what is to be avoided in a first meeting. What's key is to practice not only questions and answers, but also the format and structure of possible job interview situations—meaning how to get to the point and sell yourself convincingly and quickly.

Being prepared and knowing how to get to the point fast relates to all walks of life. And you can do so only when you know what you want.

There's a common technique for quickly summarizing yourself, called the elevator pitch, which is an excellent practice tool. You need to know how to sell yourself in the time it takes between when the elevator door opens until it closes. This means: who you are, what you want, and what is special about you or the service you can provide. By nailing this, you are prepared to meet any future job opportunity anywhere you happen to be, which may not necessarily be in an office. It could be a random opportunity in a social setting, such as at a seminar, social event, in a store, on a street corner, etc. The purpose is to create so much interest that you will be invited to a more in-depth meeting at a later time. The elevator pitch is also the backbone of your presentation in a face-to-face sit-down meeting. But in this case, the time frame I like to go by is anywhere from one to five minutes. It could be more, but the main thing is to be flexible according to your potential future employer's time. If he/she has only one to five minutes, then you better make sure to cover everything necessary in that time frame. The key is to always nail what is important.

Questions most commonly asked during a job interview Here are the eight universal questions usually asked during a job interview, followed by how to effectively answer them:

1. Please tell me/us about yourself

Answering Question #1: Focus on hard facts and what the employer needs to find out, which is, first of all, can you do the job they're interviewing you for. Talk about specific job experiences in your background that will speak on your behalf or strengthen your chances as a job candidate. Companies prefer, for the most part, to hire people who have done the same job or something similar elsewhere and have been successful at it. This is because the risk factor for someone screwing up then is very limited. So it's of very great importance in your answer or presentation to match up your experience with what the potential employer wants.

In addition, personal information about who you are is important. Everyone likes people who start out by saying where they are originally from and a little about their personal situation before they start hitting the hard facts.

Then go on to where you went to school and run through the work history. Big time gaps in work history are not good; neither is jumping from job to job if you don't have a good explanation for why.

2. What are your strong/weak points?

Answering Question #2: Many job candidates feel very comfortable when asked about their strong sides, but have a difficult time with stating weak points. If little is revealed, the trick used by many companies is to then ask, "What would your current boss say about your weak sides?" And, in almost all situations, a company that's considering hiring you will do an extensive reference check and may ask your former bosses this question.

When you are not able to answer the question about your weak points, it may be construed that you are not good at assessing yourself, when in actuality you may be hesitant because you're afraid if you are too honest you might not get the job. The truth is, everyone has flaws. As a recruiter I don't mind flaws as long as they don't affect the job in question.

Some examples of the best way to answer is by saying things such as, "I speak only English and wish I had taken time to learn another language," or "I can get too eager because I get so deep into my jobs," or "I wish I was better at public speaking in front of large groups." You may notice that these types of answers convey weaknesses that can be overcome, which is very important. The key is, your weaknesses wouldn't affect your job performance.

Bottom line, by being open you come across as a person with nothing to hide.

3. Tell me about previous managers you reported to.

Answering Question #3: A key principle is that you never talk badly about your superiors or previous superiors. First of all, there's nothing for you to gain by doing so. Even if on a personal note you feel your previous superiors were totally incompetent, saying so will only backfire and reflect badly on you. Secondly, it's a matter of showing respect. And by giving respect to others, you gain respect yourself.

Also, as a warning, I have seen companies and recruiters get so "buddy-buddy" with a job candidate during an interview that he/she drops his/her guard and speaks the total truth about a previous boss, which later in another setting boomerangs at the candidate in a negative way. To be safe, no matter what, just don't do it.

All human beings have three powerful tools: the ability to think, the ability to speak, and the ability to act. These three tools can be used to create a life of your dreams, but when not used properly, they can stand in the way of your dreams. When you are tempted to speak badly of others, understand that once those words are said, you can never take them back.

4. Where do you see yourself in the years to come?

Answering Question #4: This is also a trick question. When you have nothing to say you come across as having no aspirations whatsoever and if you speak too clearly about big plans it looks like you're going to leave the job when a better position or opportunity comes along.

The correct answer is: "My main interest is this job. I want to excel at it and do my very best. That's my objective and main focus. As far as the future, I would like to believe I will become better and better at what I do. If this means I will naturally grow into another position with this company, time will tell. But again, my goal is this job and being the best I can be in this capacity."

5. What do you know about us?

Answering Question #5: The way you answer this questions indicates whether you are prepared. It's very important to know as much as possible about the company where you are applying for a job. By being able to tell them what you know, they see that you are serious enough to have done some homework before arriving for your interview. Also, by learning as much as possible about the company, you will be able to ask the right questions and engage in an intelligent conversation about the company during your interview.

The key information to learn is the size, structure, products, services, history, the market, locations, etc., as well as details of the job you're applying for. Also know about any important events relating to the company and market it operates in, especially those covered in the media. This shows that you follow the news and stay up-to-date on what is going on in the world. Plus, you'll come across as being very smart and truly interested in the company if you can figure out what competitors the company has and how the company's products/services are different (better!) than the rest of market.

6. Why do you think you are a good match for this position? *Answering Question #6:* This is your window of opportunity to put all the hard facts on the table, convey the ways in which you are a very good match and why you are so unique. Remember, just saying you are a hard worker and a very pleasant person is a given. You need to come up with facts about what you can bring to the table that others cannot. You will be able to be specific if you have thoughtfully assessed yourself, your skills, and experience while approaching your job search. The things you say that stand out could determine whether you get the job or someone else does. Think of facts related to your skill set, your experience, a network you may have developed, or strong job-related interests that will bear fruit in the near future.

7. What is your current salary?

Answering Question #7: Talking about salary can be challenging. If the new job is for a more prestigious company and the new job tasks are more challenging, then the candidate usually says at the start of the process that the job is more important than the pay if the company is offering less. But when a job offer comes through, the candidate will usually change the story, saying something like, "But I know what I am making today and this is less." Most companies know this will happen and thereby pay attention to the salary question to make sure they are not wasting time on the wrong candidate. The reality is, everyone, including the job candidate, knows that when they made a lot more money in the past and are willing to accept a big drop in pay for this new job, they are likely to grab the next position that comes along with higher pay and jump ship. This is to a great extent understandable when someone has a number of years of experience under their belt and a certain lifestyle, expenses, and status to maintain.

But people need to look at the long term and understand that their own best interests should be driven to the greatest extent by seeking knowledge more than immediate gratification because the payoff down the road will be tremendously higher than just working for the paycheck and the ego. A hunger for more and more money is such a strong driving force that many people even go into fields/jobs/careers that don't provide them with much fulfillment besides making money.

When starting out in recruitment I was content to make not so much money because I was hungry for knowledge more than anything else. I decided that for a period of time I would rather work for less money to benefit from learning as much as possible while being part of great, positive environments. I believed that eventually the rewards would be tremendous if I pulled through and sacrificed for some years. And obviously it proved to be true.

Money should be important and you should always try to ensure you are paid market rate and what your efforts are worth. But you should never turn down great opportunities because of greed for a short-term paycheck when the long-term payoff is usually greater when you are driven by a quest for knowledge in areas where your passions can thrive.

When asked about salary, the trick is to first get the company to reveal a number. Your best approach is to just say, "If you feel I am a good fit for this company and this position, I am sure we will come to terms," or "The main thing is whether I fit the requirements of what you are looking for, and if that's so, then I would be very happy to receive an offer from you first because I am very interested in this opportunity." (Say this even if you are not.) By saying this you keep the focus on getting the job while not disqualifying yourself because of salary demands. You can negotiate a salary once you know you truly have their interest—by getting an offer, not before. If they know that in your current job you earn much more than the new position would pay, that's a different story. Then you have to decide whether taking a pay cut is worth it to you, because they're probably not going to meet or exceed your current salary.

If you know from the start of the process that the salary range of a potential new job is below what you currently earn, you need to do some soul searching to decide if you still want the job. Simply ask yourself: Will this job take me further down the road to where I want to be in my career? If so, be prepared to answer their salary question truthfully by saying, "My pay today is 'X' amount of dollars and I know what my expenses are. I am not sure what your pay range is for this position, but I want to emphasize that at this point in my life I seek to learn more and expand my skill set. This is more important to me than anything else, even if it means taking a pay cut."

On the other hand, if you have no other choice but to accept a salary cut— whether it's due to a bad economy, the chance that your current job may be eliminated, or because you are unhappy and unfulfilled in your current job— ask yourself if this may be a chance to go in a better direction in life, where you will be experiencing new values and beliefs that can help you grow and evolve. If you believe this is correct, truthfully say to the hiring company that you are venturing into new territory where you genuinely want to try something new and different, and the position in question is therefore of great interest to you.

Being honest—with yourself and your potential new employer—is the key here. Turn around and imagine you are a company that is hiring. You don't want to go through the entire hiring process and then shortly afterward see your new employee jump ship. Being honest with yourself, as well as your potential new employers, will never backfire on you.

8. What do you do outside of work, or what non-work-related interests do you have?
Answering Question #8: Companies ask a job candidate this question because most really do want to hire stable people with good, balanced lives. Incorrect answers are: "I like to hang out at the bars," or "I have no interests except for watching television." Nobody wants to hire a bar hopper or someone who spends all of their spare time glued to the television. On the other hand, having too many outside interests can give the impression they are likely to affect the quality of your work in a very negative way. I have seen numerous occasions where people say that maintaining their social life with friends is important to them— meaning their weekly outings with friends will always be more important than deadlines at work. A negative impression can also be given when people say they engage in a lot of sports activities as either a participant or a fan, because it can mean that adjusting their schedule to attend or view a sporting event can interfere with or be more important than any activity at the company.

For the correct answers, the key is to show there is balance in your life. Safe activities to talk about are: going to the gym, spending quality time with family, and going to church, the movies, or the theater, etc. Having a unique interest, such as astronomy or something else mainstream (meaning not bizarre), will always be a positive. And because most companies want employees who have stable lives, being married or having a boyfriend/girlfriend is a great plus.

How to walk, talk, dress, and look for a job interview
First impressions can get you in the door, but you also want to stay. Even before a word is spoken, you are judged by what you look like. This is human

nature. The mind and "gut feel" works so fast that within a few minutes a decision has already been made. If recruiters and potential employers could get away it, only a five-minute first meeting would be necessary—to them the remaining time too often is wasted on what is considered a wrong person, but to be polite and courteous they engage in a lengthy conversation. Most recruiters, including myself, have made up their minds about whether the person is right or wrong just by seeing them enter the hallway—before they've had a chance to say one single world. The information explained in this section can help you avoid being one of those people by understanding how recruiters and potential employers think. Keep in mind, recruiters and potential employers very often like to recruit people like themselves and, of course they want employees who will be good representatives for their company.

In my younger days, even I messed this up more than once by either saying the totally wrong things or dressing in such a bad way that I am now surprised I did those things. When I was 21 I went to the office of a leading U.S. consulting firm to apply for a part-time job wearing an off-white linen suit and a pink shirt. This was in the late eighties and the outfit was a great going out socially outfit at the time, but it was a disaster for the corporate world. I lost the job before I even got to say a word. I never once repeated that mistake because I realized what I had done. And, after all, the best way to learn is by trial and error. And looking back now, I could not have agreed more with the people who rejected me for the job.

When going for a job interview you'd better dress the part so that won't be a reason for them to reject you. How do you know what to wear? Look at the environment where you are applying for a job and dress accordingly. If you have to, do reconnaissance. Park or stand near the building where the company is located and see what types of attire the employees entering or leaving the building are wearing. Or call the company's main number and ask the person who answers the phone what the dress code or preferred attire is for those working there. Always overdress rather than under dress, but don't go so far that you're a total mismatch.

There are some universal rules that apply no matter what environment you're considering working in.
First, always dress as though you are worth what they are going to pay you. When I meet a candidate who dresses like a slacker, my first impression is

that he/she isn't worth the money being paid. And if someone doesn't have enough respect for himself/herself to dress appropriately, he/she would not be an asset in any job. As a job candidate, all you need to do is analyze the environment in which you'll be working and use common sense. When applying for a corporate job, don't come in jeans. When applying for a job in a grocery store, don't wear a dark blue suit with a tie. Always dress your part. And no matter what, you need to look sharp—neat and clean.

Next, after studying your potential new work environment and deciding what you're going to wear, put on your outfit and look at yourself in a full-length mirror. Start with your shoes. Do they look worn out and soiled? For men: Do your socks match the shoes and the pants? Are the pants clean, pressed, and in good condition? How about your belt, shirt, suit jacket, and tie, if they are appropriate? For women, do your shoes, dress, or suit look like a coordinated outfit? Are your clothes clean, pressed, and in good condition? For both men and women: Are you well put together? Does it all match and represent you? Are you proud of who you are? If so, your outfit should he appropriate and of the best quality possible.

I realize when times are tough or money is tight, you may feel overwhelmed when looking in your closet, thinking you have nothing good enough, new enough, or of the appropriate style or quality for the job you want to get. If possible, invest in yourself: go out and buy an "interview outfit." When that's not possible, borrow an outfit from a friend. The point is: This may be your opportunity to change your economic circumstances, as well as create a better job/career future, so give it your all.

Remember, for your first interview—and all other interviews to follow—always go in looking like you're ready to do the job you're applying for and will fit right in at the company. Then you'll never be judged or disqualified for the way you dress.

It's also very important to always be well groomed. Trends come and go, such as sideburns, a goat beard, or long hair on men, but one thing that never fades or changes in the professional world is looking clean cut, well groomed, and professional. In the very competitive job market, don't give potential employers any reason to kill your opportunity of getting a job just because you can't bear to part with your ponytail or goat beard (if you're a guy), claiming it's a statement about your authenticity. When you are a player in the job market you have to follow the rules in order to win.

Handshake and eye contact

A limp handshake shows no backbone. If a job candidate grasps too hard, it feels uncomfortable for the other person and give the impression he/she is trying to prove something. Perfect a handshake is warm and connecting, firm but not too hard, and engaging but not wishy-washy.

When it comes to eye contact, look your interviewer straight in the eyes throughout your meeting—unless, of course, they are showing you something, such as a report or a spreadsheet, then give it your full attention. Don't scan the room or look toward the window or down the hallway. People with wandering eyes appear to be not all the way present, which translates to "not really interested or focused." People who don't maintain eye contact also come across as being insecure, which is a liability in the work world, not an asset.

Always keep structure in a conversation

When communicating with a potential employer, in addition to being well prepared, always have a mental structure in your mind about how the meeting should and will go. In this way you can make sure everything important to you gets covered. Also, make sure to get to the point fast. If you have nothing to say, don't just talk. It's annoying. People who don't present facts or answer questions directly come across as having something to hide. On several occasions I have presented very strongly qualified and experienced candidates to clients/companies, but for some reason they couldn't get to the point. After an entire hour of social talk, not many facts were conveyed, and the clients didn't feel they learned anything about the person. In essence, the job candidates talked themselves out of job opportunities.

During a job interview conversation, always have a structure in mind and make sure everything gets covered during the allotted time. Your chances of nailing the job will increase dramatically.

Be confident, but be humble

Few companies want to hire a person who comes across as insecure. But they're also not interested in the other extreme, a person who is cocky. Nobody likes a person who is full of himself/herself. One quality every company is looking for is someone who is balanced—confident and humble at the same time.

Humor is important

In every company environment I have known, humor is key. People with a sense of self-irony are always likeable because they don't take themselves too seriously. A job environment without smiles and laughter is a horrible place to work. Little feels better than having a good laugh. Therefore, job candidates with a sense of humor are much more likeable than a dry person who has a hard time smiling. People often remember funny things that take place in the work environment, and share those stories with others. The same goes when an interviewer meets a wellqualified candidate who exhibits a sense of humor. Such a person is easy to remember.

Being able to put a smile on the face of the person interviewing you is an ice-breaker which gives you an advantage. But don't push it too far by giving the impression you don't take yourself or your job seriously— again, it's all about the balance. Nobody wants to work with a disrespectful clown. And humor can never be at someone else's expense.

Working with people as a life coach and recruiter, I have seen almost everything in regard to humorous episodes, and these events still make me smile, which fills me with happiness. Job candidates with a smile, who have the ability to connect with others, always have an advantage. And, of course, when everything else is in place they're way ahead of the game.

Physical posture in a meeting

When a job candidate enters the room for their interview with bad posture and looking uncomfortable, the impression they make is just as negative as being inappropriately dressed and unprepared. I have even seen high-profile candidates leaning back in their chairs as if they were at home in their living rooms.

It's important when you are in a job interview to sit up straight and behave as professionally as you can. And it is always more engaging if you lean forward a little toward the interviewer as it shows more interest than almost falling off the chair backwards when being too relaxed.

How to follow up after the interview

After someone takes time out of their busy schedule to meet with you regarding a potential job opportunity, it's customary and a courtesy to always send them a thank you letter or email. This letter or email is very important. It gives you an opportunity to do many things, especially when you are left with the impression that another interview or a job offer may be coming:

• Politely thank them for their time and the opportunity to meet with them about the job.
• Once again, state your strong interest in the job.
• Express that you got a great impression of their company.
• Tell them you look forward to the next step in the process.
• Also, tell them to please let you know if they need any more information from you.

Even if it was clear at the end of your interview that you and the specific job you were interviewing for weren't a good match, a thankyou letter is still needed to leave the best possible impression. Include in such a letter: thanking them for their time and what a great impression you got of their company. Also say something like: "If any future opportunities come up that may be a better match for my skills, please keep me in mind." After all, there's always a chance it could happen. And even if it doesn't, you could directly or indirectly run into that person again in the future. Always leave a good impression.

When a friend, acquaintance, someone in your network, or a recruiter has given you the job lead or set up the interview, it's important to thank them too. Thank them for the opportunity and tell them you are excited about it. If a job offer comes through, don't forget to let your contact know with another thank you. And if a recruiter arranged your contact with the company and it resulted in a fantastic job, send a gift to the recruiter. Always remember: When someone refers you for a job or hires you, they put their own name and reputation on the line. This is something to be very grateful about. Follow-ups, both after an interview and when you are hired, are critical ways to show gratitude.

When the job offer comes through: negotiating your salary Salary is part of the equation when accepting a new job. It comes down to your expectations versus those of the hiring company, as well as the marketplace. As a job applicant you want to be paid as much as possible, and on the other side the company wants to pay as little as it takes, as long as in ensures you are happy.

Determining factors will then be a mix of how much you make today or used to make, how much similar jobs in the marketplace pay, and the pay structure of the company. Sometimes negotiations can be involved to reach an agreement on a salary, while other times the numbers are so fixed that you will face a take-it-or-leave-it situation. Smaller companies may be more flexible; larger companies usually have a more fixed pay structure. Other important factors to consider are benefits: health care, 401K, insurance, company car, education benefits, etc. Even though salary and benefits are key factors in deciding whether you want to accept the job, hopefully they're not the determining factors if the numbers are close between your expectations and those of the hiring company.

Be cautious with a company that seems to be unnecessarily overpaying—it may show bad judgment, indicating it could be a highrisk company that could provide you with little job security. On the other hand, many times I have witnessed companies make a sport of paying much less than they can or should—which again is not sound long-term thinking, and it usually backfires. There is some truth in the saying: If you pay peanuts, you get monkeys. When someone is good at his/her job and is underpaid, they will leave at the first opportunity.

When entering a meeting as a job candidate you've got three choices when being asked about your pay requirements:

1) You can say "right now (or in my previous job) I make (made) X amount of dollars."
2) Say a number that is the minimum amount you want or need to get by or cover your bills if this is a job you really need and want.
3) Play hardball and state a fixed number.

Factors other than salary that may be more important to you are the working environment and the potential for where the job will take you. So, while negotiating a salary, always look at the big picture and your true objectives. Ask yourself if this is a company where you can earn enough money by being your true self and following your true passions, where you will be able to learn and grow to become all you can be. If your primary objective is earning a paycheck, it isn't necessarily a bad thing when you really need a job, as long as your expectations meet the realities of the situation. Know when accepting such a job that you must still go into work every day with the commitment of giving it 100 percent.

Making your job all it can be
The ideal is having a job/career that is fueled by your passions, enabling you

to learn and grow into being your best self while it provides more than enough financial security for you to thrive in the real world. But the reality is, sometimes it's not possible. Sometimes you just need to work for the paycheck. Even then, it's your obligation to always do the best you can do (as in every area of your life) especially if you have a job that doesn't exactly feed your passions. It's a matter of honor and a reflection of how much you truly value yourself as a person. Everything in life gets better when your belief in yourself is strong because you know you're always doing your best.

How to be successful once you are on board

Regardless of what job you are going into there are some basic rules for being successful. The first rule is to always do your best with a good, positive attitude.

The second rule is to work hard and smart. In the work world a good worker always hits it hard. Although there are some "job coaches" who tell people they don't need to work hard, just smart, in a Second Life you are always striving to be your best, including in the working world, by working both hard and smart. Therefore, you are not a person looking for shortcuts to avoid duties or expecting someone else to pick up the ball after you've dropped it or are not hitting it. There is no other way to progress except by putting in the time and effort it takes. The harder and smarter you work the better your chances of succeeding. And by doing so with a great attitude you serve as a role model for everyone else in your work environment.

In a reference check one of the questions is: Does/did he/she perform well? When the answer is that the person is/was a dedicated hard worker, then they'll get a gold star. I have never, ever meet or spoken to a company or corporation that was in great need of hiring someone lazy. The truth is, hard-working, hungry people who also work smart usually get very far in life.

Apply all of the gifts and talents of your true self to your job/career, always with a great attitude:

• Never arrive at work late, which is clearly a sign of disrespect. Better yet, arrive a few minutes before you are supposed to be there.
• Use your mind at all times to come up with new or creative ways to do your job better.
• Push yourself to finish your work and meet deadlines whenever possible,

and when necessary to work overtime needed with a smile—telling yourself
you are grateful to have this job, no matter what the job is.
• Be organized and have your work area reflect who you are and what you
stand for—which is being a role model.
• Ask for help, guidance, or assistance when you need it. No one is perfect, or
expected to be. There will always be other people who know more than you,
especially when you're new to a company. Get comfortable admitting if there
is a task or a problem you can't solve. Find out who can best guide or assist
you and respectfully ask for their help—but always within reason and when
it's not interfering with them doing their own job.
• Offer to help others. We were not brought into this world living off and by
ourselves. By lending a helping hand you're honoring the greater good—but
again, within reason and when it's not interfering with you doing your own
job.
• Be serious about your work. Take pride in your work, but don't get cocky.
Maintain and use your sense of self-irony or humor, but never at the expense
of others.
• From time to time, measure your knowledge and efficiency to make sure
you are progressing forward to new levels at all times. God wants you to
evolve in all areas of life, to grow to be all you can be. He wants you to be a
winner living at your maximum potential, which is only achieved when
working hard and smart.

I can tell you as a recruiter and on behalf of the major corporations I have
worked with, people who do these things are the ones they want to hire, and
keep as employees.

***Make a good impression from day one and you'll get a good reference
when you leave***
A determining factor for how well you do in the work world is how the
people you report to (your supervisor/boss) and your coworkers in the job
environment—both now and in the past—respond to you and perceive you.
As long as you always do your very best, follow Second Life's Four Core
Viking Traits and treat others as you want to be treated, you will be greatly
rewarded—although maybe not at the time, but for sure later down the road.
The people you interact with today, you will meet again indirectly or directly
at another time in your life. With a clean slate and good standing you can feel
confident that your back is clear.

• Don't be an underperformer. Short-sighted thinking is believing you will get away with being an underperformer. You may get away with it a few times by having good excuses, but in the long run it will come back to bite you. We are all human beings and understand that external factors can hinder our performance at work during difficult times. But this is acceptable only once or, worst case, twice. If a person bases their existence on being a mediocre performer, he or she will be red-flagged. Even if such people don't hinder better performing coworkers, they disrespect the gifts of their true self.
• Don't speak badly of others. Many people make a big mistake by speaking badly about others. People who complain about others are usually people who are not able to take responsibility for their own faults and prefer to blame someone else. Finding the negatives about others shows a person who perceives himself/herself as better than other people. Every person on the planet has negatives and positives. Assume that for the most part people are doing the very best they can, but because we are all living in our own distorted realities we don't all perceive facts the same way. Also, consider this before you speak badly of others: Perhaps you're seeing something in them that you recognize in yourself and need to correct. To me, criticism most often says more about those criticizing than those being criticized.
• Never complain about your previous bosses or coworkers. When someone complains about their previous boss/supervisor or coworkers it creates mistrust with those they're currently working with. They'll wonder what will be said about them when that person moves on. It's key to remember that your former bosses/ supervisors are the people who gave you opportunities for jobs in the past—whether or not you were able to make the most of them. Always speak (and think) in positive terms about them and be grateful for the opportunities you were given. Instead of dwelling on what could have been different or better in previous jobs, focus instead on what was good and stick with the positive thoughts.
• Criticizing your current boss/supervisor or coworkers in public is self-destructive and serves no good. In fact, it can become a huge disadvantage if word gets back to them.

A test to determine how well you're doing is simply asking yourself: How would my former and present coworkers describe me? And more importantly, would my former boss rehire me? If you answer "no" to the latter question, then any reference they might give you would not be good.

Don't take away someone else's opportunity
If someone has a job they are not grateful for, and they don't hold their opportunity and environment in high regard, that person is a rotten apple taking away someone else's opportunity. If these people cannot change their attitudes they are basically destroying everyone else's spirits by undermining the good efforts of others and keeping the right person, who would be fulfilled in their position, out of the job. Rotten apples serve no good purpose. They only spoil an environment that could be positive by limiting everyone else's growth and success.

I have worked in environments where such destructive forces have not only jeopardized the happiness of the work environment but the lives and well-being of their coworkers as well—destroying the greater good. In one particular U.S. recruitment company where I worked, every Monday morning in the elevator an employee would say, "Only five days to go, then it's the weekend." Every day it would be a countdown to the weekend. And to make it worse, there was a loud, daily countdown hour by hour. No matter how positive every worker would be, this one particular person succeeded in killing a great deal of the spirit of everyone else and, ultimately, the entire organization. These people should be removed from their work environment because they serve no good.

Don't be the rotten apple in your work environment—or in any other part of your life! While going through the process of being a job candidate, accepting a job, and once you've landed the job, ask yourself: Would you hire yourself? If you cannot make a positive contribution to the greater good and be a positive role model, don't put yourself in a position where you will be destroying the opportunities of moredeserving people—it's bad for everyone else, and it's bad for you.

View your insecurities as an opportunity for personal growth Everyone, of course, has insecurities of some kind. Many people are concerned about the impression others have of them if they are working at a job that is not considered by society's standards as acceptable or of high enough status. In other words, they are concerned about what other people think of them. When it comes to your job/career, your insecurities aren't relevant unless they affect the quality of your work— which they absolutely need not do. If you struggle with insecurities and are having a difficult time overcoming them, it's best to hide them; project confidence even if it is just role-playing.

Then, hopefully, this role being played will become so integrated that your fears and insecurities will be overshadowed, and eventually killed.

As an example, many insecure people can't accept a compliment. When someone who believes they are lacking is given a compliment, they may respond by saying, "Really?!" By doing so you reinforce the doubt you have in yourself. The next time someone compliments you, even if you don't believe it, just say, "Thank you." After saying "thank you" enough times you actually will change the way you think about yourself. This can only make you better at whatever you're doing in your job/career and create more success for everyone in your workplace and, ultimately, the company you work for.

Another way insecurity manifests itself is when someone is cocky. Regardless of how insecure you are, exhibiting a cocky attitude in the workplace means you're the bad apple that can spoil everything you touch. The difference between confident and cocky is that confident people go about their business without needing to be praised constantly for every little thing they do, and cocky people are always expressing a need to get credit for their work—which usually has the reverse effect. Having this kind of attitude creates an uncomfortable work environment and puts off your coworkers. It's not easy to diagnosis cockiness in yourself, but the next time you feel a need to require or demand to be recognized, before you do so stop and think about why you're doing it. Cocky people in a work setting must realize that in order to fit in, they need to calm down and be humble.

Every company wants to hire and keep employees who are confident and humble. If you are neither, then play the part until it becomes you. Being truly humble has been described in this way: Don't believe you know everything, as you know so little.

Create a new position for yourself

Creating a new position basically means taking on new or additional responsibilities—usually those of a coworker in order to make it easier for them to do an even better job in their core area of responsibility. Such a mindset is not just important for other people with whom you work, but also clearly shows initiative, independence, drive, and a high degree of responsibility—all traits of a person who succeeds. Taking on new responsibilities also helps you grow by learning and mastering new tasks. But such proactive conduct is beneficial only when your primary assigned job tasks have been satisfactorily completed; otherwise it serves against its purpose.

There is no reason to wait for your supervisor/boss to give you added responsibilities. Take the initiative and take on more responsibilities on your own. In most companies it's not too difficult to do. I have seldom been in a work environment where someone's efforts to take on more responsibility were restricted, as long as it does not intentionally jeopardize someone else's position. Exhibiting a good team spirit means you are concerned not only about your own job, but also the jobs of everyone around you. The most important person whose job you can make easier is your supervisor/boss. By making your boss look good, you

will also be viewed more favorably by him/her. Taking on responsibilities or tasks of a coworker may require a mindset of extraordinary stamina and drive, but you can strengthen your position and status in your current company and automatically open doors for future opportunities. The new knowledge you obtain and skills you learn could pay off with a promotion to an entirely new position in the company where you presently work, and they can be used in future jobs in other work environments.

Step Nine: Reevaluate your job/career status according to your timelines If your job/career targets are not being met according to your timelines and you've encountered roadblocks, then go back to previous steps of this job/career process to reassess what you're doing wrong. Make corrections to get yourself back on course. Then continue on your path forward toward your goal.

If all approaches you have taken to find a job or improve your current job/career situation have gotten you nowhere, go back to the drawing board and reassess your options. Review the steps you have taken. What is missing? Do you need more training or education? If you already have the necessary skills and talents, do you need an attitude adjustment? There is no surrender —which means there is always a way. The question is how.

If you know in your heart that you are doing everything right and are qualified for jobs you are seeking or advancement in your current company, you need to take more extreme measures.

When you are stuck in a job and can't make career progress, your first option is to talk with your superior. Offer to take on more responsibilities that could lead to a promotion. This, of course, requires you to take the initiative and be a good employee/role model in the company. If your supervisor says there is nothing more in the near future for you in terms of responsibilities and growth that suit your career aspirations or income needs, then it's time to plan on jumping the ship.

When you are looking for a job but can't get into the career field you've trained for or can't get a foot in the door of the companies you would like, you need to take a more targeted approach and do some smart networking.

Here's a game plan: Again, do extensive research on the companies of your choice. Ask to meet with department supervisors to interview them about exactly what they do. This will give you some ideas about what they need and you could provide. If they're definitely not hiring, and you can afford to do so, offer to provide your services to them on a part-time or project basis free of charge—so the company does not feel stuck with you. Tell them your intention is to prove to them how good you are and how you may be an asset to their team, there is no risk for them other than getting some important task/project done by you, and they can utilize your talent with no costs or other strings attached. This way, they get to know you on a personal level while you get a chance to prove how good you are. Worst case scenario, they will have nothing for you right then, but they will remember you when you follow up again later. The key is to stand out in a good way; and now you will.

Step Ten: Reassess your job/career values every six months after you are on your path
Now that you are on track, is this still what you really want? There are many ways to measure your success. One way can be to see how you are progressing by taking on new challenges to help you grow—which is a basic ingredient for feeling good about yourself because it means you are evolving. Being stagnant means the opposite. Another strong indicator of your success, which goes far beyond anything else, is the impact you have on others. This isn't necessarily a result of direct public service, but can be seen in your everyday work life—and, of course, life in general.

If you're still not where you want to be, decide what you really want. Here's a clue: Your instincts will tell you whether you are doing what you really want to do or if you are doing what you have been indoctrinated to believe you should do. Your inner voice will show you the way. All you have to do is learn to listen. You may be surprised by what you hear.

When I was around 22 years old and attending university, I got a

full-time job as a bellman in a very prestigious hotel in Los Angeles. Having the chance to work in such an environment was a huge deal for me. Employees of the hotel were treated extremely well. We had access to the same great food served to hotel guests and could stay at other hotels owned by the corporation at low rates. Although I knew this was a great work opportunity, it turned out to be a positive experience in many other ways.

Because of the nature of my job assignment as a bellman I saw instant results of my work through the interactions with the hotel guests. At the time my five-day-a-week shift started at 4:30 in the morning, which meant I got up at 3:45 to get there on time. Every morning I thanked God for having the job, being able to go to school later in the day, and being healthy. Each day I told myself it would be the best day ever. With this mindset I arrived at work happy and energized, ready to do the best job I could every day. Soon I realized that doing a good job and providing good service resulted in people giving big tips. So I'd leave work every day with a lot of extra money. I took great pride in what I did and decided to be the best possible bellman at the hotel. My next goal was to get the most recommendation cards from guests, which were then placed on a wall in the hotel. I never forget for one day how lucky I was to have the job. I felt like I was part of a great team. And never having a reason to feel down, I smiled and hit it hard, every day doing my best.

As I movedalong my path to achieve other goals I thought would give me a great feeling—to make lots of money and reach the high goals I had set—I never thoughtof my former coworkers as having lesser goals. Instead, I wanted to makethem proud of me.

Ten years later I returned to the hotel for the first time, excited to tell them how I had finally succeeded. When entering the hotel lobby I saw eight of my former coworkers. They were all smiling, genuinely happy to see me, and came over to hug me. I could tell their warm greeting came from their hearts and I was truly touched. In those moments, I realized true success was the feeling inside that I had left such a good impression that ten years later it had stood the test of time. While looking at them, laughing and smiling with them, I felt such positive energy and knew they liked me not because of what I had achieved, but because of the person I am.

Success in a job or career, as this story clearly illustrates, can be measured in many ways. We owe it to ourselves to always to do our best and be grateful for whatever jobs we have. How successful you are is greatly impacted by knowing every job is just as important as any other, and working together to make a better company.

True success at a job comes with creating positive energy, always doing your best, and being a grateful role model for others. This means mastering the four core traits; Imagination, Vision, Collaboration and Fearlessness. Together with social skills, positivity and a strong drive, you have a winning formula. From my experience as a headhunter meetings numerous job candidates over the years, I always know when I meet someone that possesses the mentioned characteristics as well as they will succeed wherever they are or go. The good news is that everyone can learn these traits, and when such stands a very good chance to become very successful in the job market.

JOB/CAREER SUMMARY

• Assess your current job/career situation.
• If it's not all it could be, identify the reasons why, such as:
- You don't have a job and need to get one.
- You're afraid you're going to lose your job.

- You want to feel more secure in your current employment or advance your position.
• Devise a game plan for recreating your job/career situation based on your new reality, including:
- Steps you will take to get a job, get a better job, secure/advance your current job, or work less in order to devote more time to the other four key areas of your life.
- Goals and objectives you will achieve.
- Timelines for enacting or making progress on your plan.
• Execute your game plan:
- Each day: Systematically set out knowing what you will do to improve, advance, or recreate your job/career situation. Follow through with commitment.
- Every night: Routinely review your accomplishments and express gratitude.
• Reassess your overall results according to your timelines:
- If you are on track, are there new goals you now want to reach?
- If satisfied with your progress and job/career status, be conscious every day of maintaining the changes you have made in order to completely wipe out your old negative programming and establish your new positive reality for the long term.
- If you have not made the progress you'd planned, go back, reevaluate your situation and find new ways to make your game plan more successful.